The Confident Homemaker: Who Told You, You Were Less Than?

by
Sugie Martin

Copyright © 2021 Sugie Martin

All rights reserved. No part of this publication may be reproduced, distributed, or transmitted in any form or by any means, including photo copying, recording, or other electronic or mechanical method, without prior written permission of the publisher, in the case of brief quotations embodied in critical review and certain non commercial use permitted by copy law. For permission request write to the publisher.

Scripture quotations are from the ESV® Bible (The Holy Bible, English Standard Version®), copyright © 2001 by Crossway, a publishing ministry of Good News Publishers. Used by permission. All rights reserved.

All rights reserved.

ISBN: 978-0-578-94659-7

Cover Design by Takima Howze
www.takimahowze.com

DEDICATION

To a woman who stood the test of challenges, pressed pass the difficult situations and raised eight amazing children - my mother Permalee Whiteley-Thomas. Since I was young, I have watched you working hard from home as a Seamstress, to make ends meet. As a single mom, you never complained. You always had a smile on your face, with an encouraging word no matter what situation you were facing. As a stay-at-home mom, you never withheld showing us love and inspiring us in any way possible that you could. As I wrote this book, it dawned on me, that I never thought that one day I too would be a homemaker like you. Thank you, Mommy, for your hard work, dedication, and the prayers you have poured over us all these years. In plain Jamaican "nof lov, lov yu bad" (love you without end).

To my wonderful Husband, Dean Martin, and my beautiful children Tahira, Samuel, Jonathan, and Malachi, Love you all. Thank you for allowing me to be a wife, mom and homemaker.

TABLE OF CONTENTS

    Dedication

    Foreword   V

1   You Are Valuable And You Are Worth More Than This   1

2   You Are Enough   18

3   Who Told You, You Were Less Than   31

4   The Courage To Be Yourself   43

5   Teach Others How To Treat You   59

6   Give Yourself Permission To Live The Life You Have Been Called To Live   73

7   Think Differently   93

8   You Are Called To Change The Next Generation   106

PREFACE

In the past, there was a stigma associated with the term 'homemakers' or 'stay-at-home moms. The Merriam-Webster dictionary defines a homemaker as "one who manages a household especially as a spouse and parent." However, being a homemaker goes far beyond managing your household and family. As well as managing goes far beyond being confined to the space or four walls of the home. The *Confident Homemaker* is a holistic view of the various roles and capacities embodied by the stay-at-home mom, her responsibilities to her family, and most of all, to herself. It speaks of balance and management as the key and the fulfillment that it will bring. It speaks of walking in dominancy and confidence in the role given, not holding back what you have to give to this world and the next generation. Therefore, as you turn the page in The Confident Homemaker "Who Told You, You Are Less Than" let me congratulate you for picking this book up to read it. I am congratulating you because you are a busy homemaker/stay-at-home mom yet, you have embarked on a new adventurous journey to live life confidently without apologies. The calling God has placed upon your life is not for the timid or the faint in heart. It is for individuals who seize the moment to live out loudly and tenaciously in the face of a society that doesn't give you the true honor you deserved.

FOREWORD BY TAMMIE T. POLK

"The CONFIDENT Homemaker"....

That's who we are MEANT to be, yet many of us fight to see ourselves that way because we allow the thoughts of others to cloud our judgment.

I love the fact that Teressa chose to take this task on to help the homemaker straighten her crown, remember who she is, and who God created her to be! While confident doesn't mean perfect, know that you are not meant to be like anyone else, nor do what anyone else does.

As you read through this book, I want you to be honest with yourself and commit to admitting, and then strengthening those grey areas of weakness you start to see. At the end of the day, the ONLY thing that matters is that you served God through serving your family to the best of your ability!

He has uniquely gifted you with a special set of talents that no one else has --- THAT makes you MORE than what anyone else thinks you are!

Even in lean times such as these, people are starting to come and sit at the feet of homemakers just like you, gleaning as much as they can to stay sane....

If THAT makes you less than... Wait! That doesn't work either!

By the time you finish reading this book, you will realize that having confidence in your God-given abilities makes you much stronger!

Become who you are MEANT to be...

Serve who you are MEANT to serve...

Do so by the grace of GOD...

Run your race with JOY!

Tammie T. Polk

Wife, Mother, and Author of over 100 books

PRINCIPLE ONE

YOU ARE VALUABLE AND YOU ARE WORTH MORE THAN THIS

Let's look at the word valuable. It means to be of great worth. Okay, if that is not enough, how about some synonyms? Beneficial, costly, expensive, helpful, important, invaluable, prized, profitable, relevant, treasured, useful, worthwhile, worthy, admired, appreciated, cherished, esteemed, estimable, high-priced, and respected.

Value is not based on what others may or may not think of you; neither is it based on the standards of the world. The standards of the world change so often; therefore, no one should base their worth on its standard. In the Bible it states in 1 Corinthians 7:23 *"You were bought with a price; do not become bondservants of men*", You are not enslaved to men's opinions or this world. If you are a born-again believer, then you are redeemed through Jesus Christ.

The principle of knowing you are valuable and your worth is a fundamental truth for every living person walking on this earth. As homemakers knowing your value and worth helps you to serve your family and others extraordinarily. When we look through the lens (value and worth) of the world, we mess ourselves up and walk out of alignment with God's word.

Think about it like this—every day you wake up and turn on the TV, you will be bombarded with something that says that what you do daily is wrong. Eight hours of sleep is too much. This diet or exercise regimen isn't going to work for you. Stop eating this. Don't eat that. Lose weight this way! Listening to all that mess will have you scared to wake up the following day. It's all about making money and has NOTHING to do with helping you to fulfill who God created you to be as a person. If you live your life trying to follow the world's standards, you will always be in the wrong because the standards change on the hour! As a stay-at-home mom, you will be made to feel as though you are valueless because you chose to put your family first. You will be told that you are worthless or you have little ambition. Let me share with you something that a friend told me that her pastor said: "Two hundred years ago, everyone was at home!" Being a stay-at-home mom is nothing new - we're just acting like it is! International number one Motivational speaker Les Brown quoted this "If you don't program yourself, life will program you!" In other words, when we as homemakers allow the thoughts of how others devalue our position of choosing to stay home to get into our minds, it begins to program how we behave towards ourselves and others.

Isn't it ironic that during the COVID-19 pandemic, many of us were being forced to stay at home? During economic distresses and loss of jobs, many were forced to stay at home. But, you chose to believe in yourself way before a pandemic to nurture your family by offering your time, knowledge, and skills to improve them and yourself.

My mother stayed at home and raised eight (8) of us in a culture that didn't embrace women staying at home. As a seamstress, she worked tirelessly to ensure we had food on the table while most females worked outside the house. Additionally, my mom was a single mother. I can recall as a child hearing other people talking about her in a devaluing manner because she chooses to stay-at-home and raise her eight (8) children. I can recall persons saying, "why does she have so many children?" "Where is the father?" I know things were not easy for my mother, especially because she was a single mother, but Mom decided to block out whatever was said about her and move forward.

My friend's mom became a stay-at-home mom at an early age and couldn't handle it because she had no support from her husband, whom she expected to support her decision. She went through unimaginable abuse, crippling her self-esteem and self-worth. Despite all that was happening, she ensured that her children were taken care of, but it was at the expense of her peace of mind.

After the marriage ended, she went into the workforce but had no peace as a factory worker. It took her oldest son getting into trouble at school and getting expelled for her to finally embrace the path that led to her rediscovering her value. This did not happen without criticism from those who called themselves her friends.

While everyone focused on her struggles; she was determined to climb! What you need to understand is that it took everything within her to press through. As Linda Wooten said, "being a mother is learning about strengths you didn't know you have."

Whatever brought you to being home full-time, understand that there is a reason for it! During the pandemic we are all faced, many women have found themselves being forced to stay home because of the COVID-19. This position was like a 'rock-and-a-hard-place' for moms who have never thought of staying home with their children. Most Jobs, Schools, daycares, parks, and recreation places have been closed. The thought of juggling working from home with children making circles around you is frightening, especially where video meeting calls are concerned. Although staying at home was not anticipated, adjusting your frame of mind is critical in helping to maneuver the deep waters of this incredible journey ahead of you.

The first thing you need to understand is that you must take care of yourself first! The Lord has given you a fantastic job to do on this earth and to do so; you need to understand that when Jesus paid the price for you, you no longer live for yourself; *"For the love of Christ controls us, because we have concluded this: that one has died for all, therefore all have died; 15 and he died for all, that those who live might no longer live for themselves but for him who for their sake died and was raised"*, (2 Corinthians 5:14-15). I know in our culture or society, many promote self-development to glorify oneself. This is not the perspective I wish to highlight. We are not called to lift ourselves but to lift the one who called us. Christ is expecting us to take care of the temple he as entrusted within our care. As a homemaker, you may often neglect to take care of yourself in the process of looking after the family and others. Yes, I understand that you want the best for your family and that you are pouring yourself into them every day. But are you pouring from an empty cup? If you are, then you need to stop. When you pour from an empty cup, that means you have lost your purpose and focus!

So often, I hear homemakers saying, "But I don't feel valuable…". Then, that is something that you need to work on. God never intended for you to be miserable and frustrated during your season of building your family. It is meant to be a joy; however, when you forget to develop yourself and focus on God's word while developing your family, you will remain in that unhappy state for an extended period of time! You will start to resent your family because they are enjoying their life, and at the same time, resentment is building up in your heart.

When my mom was happy, we were happy; when she was upset or in a bad mood, it showed on every one of us.

You are valuable because God says you are! How so? You are not your past mistake, you are not your failures, you are not your weaknesses, nor are you, men's opinions. First, my love, you are made in the image and the likeness of God Himself! NO MATTER whose image you try to craft yourself into, you could not have been made, nor could you be made any better than that! Every inch of you is unique and, even if you have a twin, you are still vastly different from them and any other person on Earth.

Having a relationship with you is so important to God that, when Adam and Eve sinned in the Garden, He came up with a plan to get you back. Yes, you have had to deal with much to get back into fellowship with Him but know that it was His plan to have you back in His arms from the beginning. He gave you the Bible to show you what He has done and will do for you throughout your relationship with Him if you will only trust Him! Being Bible-based does not mean being religious, restricted, or redundant. Being Bible-based is to be free and to live in the freedom that Christ dies for you to have. You will see that trusting in Christ and living in the Bible is more liberating than anything else. Besides, the Bible is where most of these motivational speakers get their quotes and wisdom. They just tweak it to sound differently.

Your value was set by a loving God Who didn't want you to be alone, so He blessed you to have a family to love and cherish but not for you to lose yourself! You may see the need to put your family first. However, you must understand that there will be times when they will need to take a second-row seat! Because

You are more than a nanny…

You are more than a maid…

You are more than a cook…

You are more than a chauffeur…

You are more than a bedroom companion…

You are a woman on a mission from God to live the absolute best life that you can according to God's blueprint. But, first, you must take care of yourself, and the first part of that is realizing that you are valuable and that you have something rare and precious to offer the entire world – not just your family! Did you hear me? I said, "what you have is not just for your family but for the world to experience."

While reading the Daily Bread one morning, the actions of this mother got a hold of my heart:

Singer/songwriter Robert Hamlet wrote "Lady who prays for me" as a tribute to his mother, who made a point of praying for her boys each morning before they went to the bus stop. After a young mother heard Hamlet singing his song, she committed to pray for her little boy. One day after her son went out the door, he returned, bringing kids from the bus stop with him five minutes later! His mom asked what is going on? The boy responded, "their moms didn't pray for them."

What lasting impact will you have on another individual? Therefore, when you look in the mirror in the morning, take time to look for whom your father sees you as and not what others may perceive. Besides, when you look in the mirror again, ensure you remind that beautiful lady you are looking at of these few words:

"...I am a new creation. The old has passed away; behold, the new has come" (2 Corinthians 5:17 (ESV))

"For I am Christ workmanship..." (Ephesians 2:10 (ESV))

"I am a Child of God" (John 1:12 (ESV))

"I am the light of this world" (Matthew 5:14 (ESV))

"I am fearfully and wonderfully made" (Psalm 139:14 (ESV))

"I am the Apple of God's eye" (Psalm 17:8 (ESV))

You are valuable and blessed beyond measure because you have gifts, talents, and strengths that no one else has! But, there is something that only YOU can do in this world! That's why you can't hang out with every mom around you. That's why you only have a few close friends. That's why you seem crazy to those who refuse to understand how a woman who chose to stay at home can do so with JOY!

You are worth more than what they say because they don't have the final say over your life! Job said it best when he said, "Though He slays me, yet will I trust HIM!" God takes you through these valleys for you to learn to trust Him!

So, when you stand before that mirror saying that you're too pale or too dark, that you hate the way you look, etcetera, stop and say that there are things out there that will enhance your physical beauty, and you will look a thousand times better than what this hostile world will have you to believe. What they tell you will pale in comparison to the beauty that comes from committing your thoughts, ways, and actions to God first and letting Him lead and guide you to what will work for you. Yes, He will even lead you into something like that!

He will show you what you can eat to give you the same glow as any beauty product could. He will show you what He created in nature that will bring you the look that you want. He will show you how to use what He has given you to help others. He will show you your true value! You will learn what it truly means to see yourself as valuable.

The gifts that He has given you will carry your home through rough times. The tenacity and strength that you gain from allowing HIM to lead you will cause your children to have faith in God and come to know Him for themselves. This world won't mean anything to you anymore…it won't be able to touch you! You will look at those news reports, laugh, and say, "Oh, really? We'll see what MY GOD has to say about that!"

As you read through the rest of this book, you will understand exactly what I mean by the title of this chapter. Think of it as a step-by-step instruction manual for you to put the pieces of your life together in order to build the woman that God ordained you to be!

It's Your Time Now, Mama!
Copy this truth once a day and scream it out loud.
TRUTH: I am valuable because God made me valuable!

"You shall be a crown of beauty in the hand of the Lord, and a royal diadem in the hand of your God." Isaiah 62:3

_____

_____

_____

_____

_____

_____

Ephesians 1:4

_____

_____

_____

_____

_____

1 Corinthians 6:20

_____

_____

_____

_____

2 Corinthians 1:21

_____

_____

_____

It's Your Time Now, Mama!
Unload your personal thoughts and reflections.

_____

_____

_____

_____

_____

_____

What special insight have you received through scriptures about what God has said about you?

How do you sense the Lord is speaking to you about trusting Him in leading you on this path of being a Homemaker?

_____

_____

_____

_____

_____

_____

_____

_____

_____

_____

_____

_____

_____

PRINCIPLE TWO

YOU ARE ENOUGH

Many homemakers are living under guilt and condemnation because they choose to stay home with their family. Why is this so? For years, I lived under an umbrella of low self-worth. Before getting married, I was an independent woman who enjoyed working in the corporate world. I was rock solid on who I was and what the rest of my life would look like. Over several years, after staying home with my children, I became more settled and started to compromise who I am. Unfortunately, I got stuck in the rut of the mundane things in life, not realizing that my dreams and desires had been swept under the carpet like dust.

It is so easy to watch life pass us by because we get so occupied or locked into our own little world. We have allowed society to put a stamp on us and derail us. They push who we genuinely are into a corner because we are not working outside of our homes.

I used to look at the expression of people as they ask me, "what do I do for a living?" When I responded, "I am a homemaker," their expression would always change in a manner that is puzzled and unpleasant. The response is, "oh, ok." It is funny to note how the wheel is changing, and more persons have no other choice but to become a homemaker, both females and males alike. If someone had told them that they would have become a stay-at-home parent the previous year, I am so sure their conversation would not have gone well. Needless to say, God already knew this would have happened. "For I know the plans I have for you," declares the Lord, "plans for welfare[a] and not for evil, to give you a future and a hope.." (Jeremiah 29:11). When God has a plan for you, He will ensure his purpose comes to fruition. He knows your children need you in these uncertain times so that they can feel more secure and safe. He knows they need extra affirmation to get them through their last year of high school. He knows they need you to be present so that there is more cohesiveness in the home. And He knows your babies need you to spend more time sharing His word each day with them.

Are You Showing up Well?

Many years ago, while attending a Christmas dinner with my husband, I will never forget one of his co-workers asked me, "So, what is it that you do?" With a big smile, my response was, "Oh, I just stay home with the children." You should have seen the look on their faces. Instantly, I imagined that the ground opened under my feet, and I disappeared. For the rest of the evening, I stood with a sweet smile on my face and listened to each individual chat away. It was at this moment that I realized that things needed to change in my life. I made a vow in my heart that this would not happen to me again. You might be asking yourself, "what will she not allow to happen to her again?"

Well, it is how we respond when we are asked, "what do we do?" What was taking place is that I allow individuals to make me feel as those I was not enough. And in doing so, I step out of alignment with the principle of You are enough. When you know you are enough, no one will be able to intimidate you or make you feel less than. So, when anyone asks what you do, does your response come out confidently or timidly? When you fully embrace who you are and whom you are created to be, the principle of You are Enough will show up in your attitude, smiles, and posture. At no time should we be ashamed or fearful of what we are called to do and accomplish. Raising your family, keeping our home together, and providing an enriched environment, are more than enough. Society has put a stamp on stay-at-home moms and dads for a long time, but we are the ones that allow them to do so. It is how we present ourselves to others. I know many of us present ourselves in a 'whatever kind of way', as if we don't even put a value on what we are doing or who we are. Yet, we have one of the most extraordinary tasks on this earth – to raise children for the kingdom of God, to raise respectable citizens, to raise individuals who will not be led astray by bullies or the kingdom of darkness. Let me just say you don't need men's approval to be enough. *"For am I now seeking the approval of man, or of God? Or am I trying to please man? If I were still trying to please man, I would not be a servant of Christ."* (Galatians 1:10).

Other people's opinions are not critical! You were who you are way before they had an opinion. What others portray does not match up to how God made and sees us. We have bought into the lies of who we should be rather than who we truly are. We are valuable, and we are enough!

Let's look at this from a different angle by looking through a magnifying glass. What was your family, friends, or even acquaintances' expressions when you told them you were going to stay home with your children?

Was there excitement in the atmosphere?

Did they say, "I am so excited for you," or "Oh, my gosh, this is awesome"?

I bet that most of you reading this book have a look on your face like, "Yeah, right." The point is, if they didn't have an "I am so happy for you" look or say, "That is the best decision you have made for your children," then you should still be excited about your choice. If we depend on others to show us their approval of our choices, then we are living on the wrong planet!

When I resigned from my job and decided to stay home with my daughter, who is now sixteen years old, it was not well received.

In my hometown, females are very independent and must go out and work. They worked their tails off to achieve anything they desired. Therefore, it was expected of me to do the same thing, but God had a different plan for my life.

This notion of "a woman needs to go to work" caused many arguments in my marriage. My husband was okay with me staying home, but he often gets a backlash from his family. Yet, through it all, we stood our ground, and here I am today, proudly staying home with our four children.

If those around you don't support the season you are in, you need to move on and let them be. You have been called to a higher position in Christ Jesus to accomplish a task that is not common to everyone.

"Brothers, I do not consider that I have made it my own. But one thing I do: forgetting what lies behind and straining forward to what lies ahead, I press on toward the goal for the prize of the upward call of God in Christ Jesus." (Philippians 3: 13-14). Accepting the calling to be a Homemaker in this season of your life is important. Know that who God has called, He equips. Therefore, YOU are enough. As it is with the natural seasons in

life—Summer, Autumn, Winter, and Spring – it is with us as stay-at-home moms.

Whether you are forced to stay home or choose to stay home, embrace your season just as you would have to embrace the Winter or Spring season and remember YOU are enough!

It's Your Time Now, Mama!
Copy this truth once a day and scream it out loud!
TRUTH: I am enough because God is enough and has given me all I need!

2 Corinthians 9:8

"And God is able to make all grace abound to you, so that having all sufficiency[a] in all things at all times, you may abound in every good work."

_____

_____

_____

_____

_____

_____

_____

_____

You are made in the image of God and you are more than Enough! which of these below is most important in identifying what is important to God.

- Faithfulness
- Appearance
- Integrity
- Myself
- Character
- Wardrobe
- Trusting oneself
- Popularity

Add your own list of what you might think is important to show you are more than enough!

_____

_____

_____

_____

_____

_____

_____

Go ahead and declare

"But you are a chosen race, a royal priesthood, a holy nation, a people for his own possession, that you may proclaim the excellencies of him who called you out of darkness into his marvelous light." 1 Peter 2:9

_____

_____

_____

_____

_____

_____

_____

_____

_____

_____

_____

_____

_____

_____

_____

It's Your Time Now, Mama!
Unload your mind and then pray about it!

PRINCIPLE THREE

WHO TOLD YOU, YOU WERE LESS THAN?

Who told you, you were less than? In asking yourself this question, you are able to realign yourself with the principle of **'You are more than enough**!' In 1 Peter 2:9

"But you are <u>a chosen race</u>, a royal priesthood, a holy nation, a le for his own possession, that you may proclaim the excellencies of him who called you out of darkness into his marvelous light"

God has chosen you and everything you need to walk through this journey on earth.

I have come across so many women who say, "You're a stay-at-home mom? Girl! I couldn't do that because I'd go crazy!"

"I wish I could sit at home and do nothing all day."

"Being at home is good, but you need a real job."

If you're honest, you've lost count as to how many times you've heard these very same things. Inside, you become angry because people see you as "just a mom." They don't see how you're up when they're sleeping, the work at home that you do, nor how tired you are. But, then, they have the audacity to both think and say that you don't work. They don't see the value in what you do and make you feel as though you don't do anything at all…

Let me ask you a critical question—**Who told you, you were less than?**

"Less than what?" You may ask.

Less than a woman because you chose to be home with your children.

Less than a "real" woman because you don't work and make your own money.

Less than who God made you to be because you use the gifts, and talents He gave you to uplift your home and keep things running smoothly.

Less than them because they view making money as the only factor of true success.

Listen to me very carefully – GOD DID NOT MAKE YOU LESS THAN ANYTHING OR ANYONE ON THIS EARTH! Whether you think so or not, you are here for a divine reason and that's all you should be concerned about.

Less than? Hmph! Let me tell you what the Bible says about you, my dear.

First, I want you to know that you were made in the image of God Himself, so you should already know and understand that you are nowhere near less than! He created you just the way He needed you to be for you to do what He has asked you to do as an essential part of your home *"So God created man in his own image, in the image of God he created him; male and female he created them."* (Genesis 1:27).

And if that passage of scripture was not enough to show you that you are not less than, then look closely at what David said in the Psalms: *"Your eyes saw my unformed substance (body); in your book were written, every one of them, the days that were formed for me, when as yet there was none of them."* (Psalm 139:13-16). WAIT! did you see that God saw your unformed body way before it was even knitted into your mother's womb? And in addition, all your days were written before one of them even came into existence? Just stop for a moment and think upon these words of the scripture.

Second, you were created because you are needed! When God looked at Adam, He wanted him to have the same relationships the animals had, so he put Adam to sleep, took a vital piece – a rib, which protects his heart, and created Eve because he needed HELP! You were created because people need you. They may never admit it or acknowledge it, but they do need you.

Third, God values you so much that He spends a great deal of time in the Bible telling your husband or partner how to treat you! Would He do that if you were less than or unimportant? I don't think so! He did it because you are a precious treasure that needs to be cared for. Men and others around us do things to make us forget this, so I'm here to remind you that you are NOT less than.

Fourth, God in His Word gives us examples of women who knew what it meant to take care of home. He shows us the good, bad, and ugly; however, the women we know about moved mountains and birthed whole nations! The children of these women were mightily used of God, and as their mothers, they were highly spoken of for it! Think of women such as Jochebed (the mother of Moses), Sarah (the mother of Isaac), Hannah (the mother of Samuel), Mary (the mother of Jesus) etc.

Let me stop right here for a minute. I want you to realize that being a mother and a homemaker is a gift! So many women balk at us because they want to be where we are but can't right now because of things going on in their lives.

It also could be that they were once but allowed others' opinions to sway them to leave their home, and now they're stressed out.

And on the flip side, some women who swear they would never become homemakers suddenly either see the need to become one or have no other choice but to become one.

I also want you to think about other homemakers around you. They, like you, had or may have had lucrative careers that they walked away from to take care of their home.

These women were lawyers, doctors, nurses, government officials, and the like.

They made a conscious decision to walk away because their home was more important to them. There's nothing worse than being successful at work and unsuccessful at home. So, they walk away because their family is worth more than that to them. They are worth more than that to themselves.

So, you're not less than if you choose to walk away to save your home. You decided not to throw money at the problem, thus working yourself into the ground so that you can keep it up. You looked at what is going on in your home, said enough was enough, prayed about it, and stepped out in faith, armed with the promises of God.

I remember a dear friend telling me her story. She told me that, when she made her decision, her boss told her that she hadn't prayed about it, that she would struggle, and that she'd be begging her back for her job. None of that happened!

But then you may say that's not you because you decided from the start.

Maybe you married young and started your journey at home. But, you're still not less than! That means you took the time to build your home and nurtured it in anticipation of having a family.

You've done something outside for a short time to fulfill a need quickly, but still, you've been home for the most part.

Whichever state you're in, I want you to understand that you are not less than. I keep saying that because I want you to feel it in your soul. I want you to realize that as God's daughter, you are valuable to Him most of all. Never forget that He would've done all that He's done for you had you been the only person in the world! He loves you and has blessed you to be where you are. Be obedient to Him, and you will start to see yourself for whom He made you truly to be. **You are more than...**

A career

Money

A life of prestige

A title

A company

An award

A house

There is something that needs to spring forth from you that won't unless you are where God needs you to be. I'm glad you made a choice to get there before He put you there!

Let the world laugh and let your family talk because talk is all it is. Then, at the end of the day, you can rest in the fact that you are doing what God has asked you to do. You are not less than because you put God and your home first.

Putting God first is some people's biggest problem. They'll make you feel like you're less than because you follow God's path for your life, which, in today's world, is an unpopular thing to do. Just remember that no one and nothing that you're doing can give you what God can give you for true happiness, growth, and success that comes from Him.

You chose to be a Confident Homemaker, and that makes you more than. Pleasing the Lord is your sole focus, and you show that through how you manage your home. You're not less than because you want to have a Godly home, marriage, children, and relationships. You are more than because you know and understand that you are a steward that must give an account to God for what He's entrusted you to take care of. You are more than because you realize that the church, school, and government should not and cannot run your household, so you stand up, breathe, roll up your sleeves, and get things done. So, again, I ask you, *"who told you-you were less than?"* They lied to you!

They said it because they see the joy that you have even in the midst of a trial.

They're jealous because they may make twice as much as you do, but you have more.

They reluctantly come to you for advice because you have a better handle on life.

They have a sickening feeling on the inside because they see the harmony you have established in your home.

They realize that they could very well have all that you have but refuse to take that first step because they're more concerned about pleasing men more than God.

They stay away from you because they can't stand the sight of the blessings of obedience.

They realize that you are more than.

So, praise God, keep going, and tell yourself that you are more than what they think, believe, say, or tell others. You are the daughter of a King…act like it!

It's Your Time Now, Mama!
Copy this truth once a day and scream it out loud!
TRUTH: I am not less than because God gave me strength and power!

(Daniel 2:23) "To You, O God of my fathers, I give thanks and praise, For You have given me wisdom and power; Even now You have made known to me what we requested of You"

_____

_____

_____

_____

_____

_____

_____

_____

_____

It's Your Time Now, Mama!
Unload your mind and then pray about it!

_____

_____

_____

_____

_____

_____

_____

_____

_____

_____

_____

_____

_____

_____

_____

_____

PRINCIPLE FOUR

THE COURAGE TO BE YOURSELF

What will it take for you just to be YOU?

When you were created, God ensured He did not make a mistake by creating a second person like you.

I often see people trying to imitate someone famous or someone they admire.

But, how long can you really do so?

The courage to be yourself is a principle that every individual on this earth should apply. It comes with the boldness and tenacity just to be you, whether you are accepted by anyone else. In using this principle, being confident will be a natural way of life.

When you look in the mirror each day, speak to that person you see and tell yourself:

"I love you!"

"I am beautiful!"

"I am strong!"

"I am elegant and flawless!"

If you are not able to say these words to yourself, something is wrong. Loving yourself is the first step in loving someone else. Before you can fully love yourself or anyone else, you must first learn how to accept the love of God for yourself!

The truth is this: God loves you just as you are, faults and all because he knows whom He created you to be.

Knowing that someone can love you for who you are, frees you to do the same for yourself. It allows you to extend the same grace to others.

Being able to accept whom you are created to be is huge! When you see who God is and the care that He has taken to create you so uniquely, you can't help but treasure what He treasures.

Sometimes I look in the mirror, laugh, and say, "I just love me!" Why do I do that? Well, it gives me joy! I have come to realize that the world is a dark place and not everyone in it will be kind to this body that God has given to me. Therefore, I first must be kind to myself because I am a gift from God!

When you are kind to yourself and others see that you have that love, they will gravitate toward you and want to be around you all the time. Why? They are attracted to how you treat His treasure.

They can see that what God has created is worth nurturing.

They will know that you will nurture who they really are – not the image they have made of themselves – in the same way, because their true selves are also created and treasured by a loving God. When being yourself becomes a non-negotiable, it's an incredible feeling.

Another thing you need to accept is that you are flawless and beautiful! Girl, the world's description of beauty is distorted.

They only look at the outward appearance of a woman and not the inner beauty of her character.

They attach beauty to a skinny woman with a large bust and a narrow waist. I respect all ladies out there who look that way, and don't get me wrong, you are beautiful; however, if a woman bases her beauty on such description, then there are many ugly females walking around!

The word of God says that we are made in the image and likeness of God and that God fearfully and wonderfully makes us.

A friend's aunt didn't understand how beautiful she already was. Every day, she watched women on TV, looking for someone to pattern her life after. She found Alexis Carrington, a character from the show "Dallas." At that moment, she said, "That's it! That's who I want to be!" She styled her hair like hers, dated the same kind of men, dressed the same way, raised her children the same way – she even went as far as to have bones removed from her feet in order to continue to wear high heels after her doctor told her she could no longer wear them.

After a while, she wasn't happy with who she saw in the mirror, nor was she happy with her life! Now, because of all that she's done to her body, she is going blind, can barely stand wearing shoes, and is suffering from short-term memory loss and migraine headaches, which sometimes require surgery to ease.

If she was being true to who she really was, there would be no room for her to try to be like someone else. In essence, she was not authentic and being herself. Having the courage to be yourself is showing you are authentically and unapologetically you – not caring what others may or may not think of you and living it out loudly.

Now, we live in a world with so much falseness and fakeness. If at any moment we think of being ourselves, there is so much to compete with. Our life has become a platform through the windows of Facebook, Instagram, Twitter, television, etc.

There is enough pressure for any woman, not just a stay-at-home mom, to feel intimidated and not up to the challenge of being themselves.

Is it that homemakers have allowed society to invade their minds, paralyze them, and stop them from being bold and fearless?

I know there are many challenges with social media and, if you are one of those moms who is often engrossed in social media, then you'll soon see the truth. Unfortunately, the majority of what you may see in the media is not a true reflection of reality. A person only puts their best selves out there online because they fear being rejected or criticized for showing their authentic selves.

I know it is not easy to embrace what you may call flaws and weaknesses. You fear that others may not accept you for who you are; however, you'll see the endless opportunities for enjoying who you are when you dare to be yourself. As you learn new things about yourself that you would not discover by trying to be someone else, you'll find that being yourself is priceless! Being yourself naturally pulls others towards you and helps to teach others how to treat you. I will unpack this in the next chapter.

Imagine for a moment that you have reached the age of seventy-five, and it finally dawns on you that you lived your whole life being faithful to pleasing others. Instead, you spent a whole lifetime behind a mask. At this point in your life, time cannot be reversed, and most of the people you have tried to please are nowhere to be found.

How would you feel, and what would you do?

Ladies, I promised myself years ago that I will not live my life in regret nor will I live my life solely to please others.

As I come to the end of this chapter, there are a few things I did differently after coming to this verdict.

I ALIGNED myself with my values. The word value can be defined as our personal conviction or what we believe to be essential and desirable to us.

What are the values that govern your life?

Everyone has their own values, and when you understand yourself, it is an integral aspect of how you make decisions. These are the same values we instill in our children as they grow. However, as the years progress and we become homemakers, those values we hold so dearly to us sometimes fade away, and thus, we become more passive. Let me explain some more.

Remember how, at first, you ensured that most of the decisions you made were without asking others' opinions or even second-guessing yourself?

Now, you constantly seek the praises of others or always ask for their opinion.

You dismiss your values and mistrust your own standards just to please others.

You may know what you want to do, but you throw it out the window because of someone else's opinion. If I am talking to you, you need to evaluate yourself and decide to regain your posture to become who you truly are. I know you know what you want, so quit sidestepping! Move into action and treat your own values with respect or no one else will.

Secondly, the thing you need to ALIGN yourself with is Freedom. If you regain your posture and have an inner conviction of your value, then you will be free to be yourself.

Let's look at the word freedom. Freedom is the power or right to act, speak, or think as one wants without hindrance or restraint. True freedom comes from within!

Giving others the upper hand in your decisions and not allowing yourself to freely speak your mind will lead to you living in bondage. We are all called to be self-governed, not to be entrapped by others.

Let me tell you about this homeschool mama in my circle of friends.

She is a married, homeschooling mother of 5 and a pastor's wife.

She's ALSO an author, coach, and speaker who runs a nonprofit helping women.

She hides NOTHING!

She does lives on Facebook unfiltered.

She will literally be cooking, cleaning, feeding her baby, changing diapers, etc., during her live shows.

Her hair isn't always done; she's not always dressed up.

None of that!

But she is living a life of freedom without having to consult with others on what she should or shouldn't do. There are no barriers and no hindrances in her mind. She knows her value and sticks to it no matter what others may or may not think of her.

When you have a posture of not running to family or friends each time you make a decision and look within, you'll see what you desire and bring that freedom you need to live out your own values.

Finally, who are you ALIGNING yourself with? The individuals within your circle should be those who cherish and love who you are and not trying to change directly or indirectly who you are.

I get it; if you stand for nothing, you will fall for anything. In other words, if you don't make your value known, or live it out loud, then you will just go with whatever comes along without questioning it.

Your circle of friends should and must be the type of people who will always uplift you and encourage you. If you are around people that are not doing so, then dash like Usain Bolt, or run like Forrest Gump – and keep running! If you have not watched that movie, get some popcorn and sit and watch it.

In essence, run away from people who do not add to your life. We all need healthy relationships to stand firm in the world.

Therefore, it is important to ensure your friends are aligned with your value and freedom to be who you are called to be.

It's Your Time Now, Mama!

Copy this truth once a day and scream it out loud!
TRUTH: I am ME because God fearfully and wonderfully made ME!

_____

_____

_____

_____

_____

_____

_____

_____

_____

_____

_____

_____

_____

_____

_____

_____

_____

_____

_____

List your non-negotiable about being yourself!

_____

_____

_____

_____

_____

What are the values that govern your life?

It's Your Time Now, Mama!
Unload your mind and then pray about it!

PRINCIPLE FIVE

TEACH OTHERS HOW TO TREAT YOU

One day, as I began my daily routine with the children, I was bombarded with phone calls, texts from other people, and tasks from my to-do list.

I often respond immediately to their requests, but something wasn't right in my spirit this time around.

I thought to myself, "Most of these calls and texts are from friends and family who are either at work, taking their break or it is convenient for them at the time."

When I took a few minutes to myself during my children's lunch break, I came to the realization that it's my fault they didn't respect my time. The principle of teaching others how to treat me was not establish at all. These individuals knew we homeschooled from 9 AM to 3 PM, yet still, they thought little or nothing of it to call during those times. Mind you, these were not emergency requests, but things that could wait until I was free.

In the past, I would jump at their beckon and interrupt the flow of my day or whatever I was doing at that moment. But, in doing so, I was teaching them how to treat me as it related to my time.

Another example is in how we introduce ourselves. Oh, this is a big one!

Many years ago, I was intimidated by people with high positions in their secular jobs. For example, I was at a function with my husband at the university where he works. As usual, someone would introduce themselves and tell what they do. When it was my turn, I would say, "Oh, I just stay home with the children." Immediately, I was looked at like, "Oh, she just stays home." This used to hurt so badly.

During the rest of the conversation, I would just smile and nod my head, but inside was like, "Really? You think I am unaware of your dismissal of who I am?".

Another cute remake I get several times is "I could never do that"—like it takes rocket science to stay home and love on your family, nurture your children, be present in every given moment, make fun-filled memories, etc. Or are they saying it is demeaning to stay home? I am still trying to figure out that statement; however, whatever their reason for not staying home with their beautiful children is their business.

Looking back on this situation, I can clearly say I didn't answer confidently when I was asked that question.

As the years progressed, I came to realize that the way I answer the question when it is asked is important. Now, when someone asks what I do, my response is NOT "Oh, I just say home with my children. It is "I am a Homemaker and a Life Coach for Homemakers who are ready to live their life intentionally!" My posture makes a huge difference.

Ladies, you are not just staying home with your children; you are doing more than that.

You are shaping world changers, entrepreneurs, government leaders, presidents, and more.

You know the art of multi-tasking and you make thousands of decision in a day.

You are the CEO of Domestic Affairs!

Do not think for one minute that you are the underdog because you stay at home with your children.

It's about time you start to apply the principle of teaching others how to treat you.

Teach them how to always value your time as well as show you respect. It doesn't matter the field you are in—you are a cut above the rest of the individuals surrounding you.

Once while at a retreat with my family, I was in a circle of ladies who were standing around talking about what they do and how things are changing around us.

I remained quiet until one of them asked, "How are you?"

I replied, "I am doing very well! Thanks for asking."

She began to compliment me on how well-mannered my children were and knew my husband was a chemistry professor, but she wasn't certain of what it was that I did.

I responded, "I am a Homemaker and a Life Coach for Homemakers who are ready to live their life intentionally!" They all looked at me with eyes wide open and started trying to ask me questions simultaneously. I began to laugh and then proceeded to answer them one at a time.

Later that night, one of the ladies approached me and asked for help in an area of her life she'd been stuck in for a while. I spoke with her for about thirty minutes and advised her on the steps she should take.

She needed to ensure her boundaries were in place so others would not have the audacity to walk all over her anymore. A year later, we went back to the annual family retreat, and she was excited to share how things are different because she implemented what I told her. This woman realized she was allowing others to walk all over her because she chose to stay home with her children.

Posture has a lot to do with how we project ourselves. For example, when we first thought of staying home, some of us were so excited. But some, on the other hand, were not at all.

For those who were excited, someone along life's journey might have said something negative about staying home and, because of this, it causes you to think less of the position God has given to you. You have taken on the world's viewpoint instead of honoring the position you have been given. It is so easy to follow the crowd and not to stand out and have your own position.

Before becoming a stay-at-home mom, I used to hear all about the moms who stay home all day and do nothing. They wouldn't even lift a finger in the house, and the children were out of control or didn't even get a good meal. Laundry is undone, and dishes are always in the kitchen sink. Because of their lazy unacceptable posture, society took this information and spread it like wildfire.

Thinking about this toxic behavior has led to mistreatment of those who genuinely stay home and take care of their family and even run their own businesses, too.

The old way of thinking is still stuck in society's minds, and thus, homemakers must stand up, reposition themselves, and be confident in who they are!

It is time you start talking yourself into the proper posture.

Refrain from looking down on the high position God has given to you and stop allowing others to invade your mind.

Speak to yourself and start to declare the right words over posture. Start to say things like, "I am a proud stay-at-home mom. I love staying home with my children. It is a delight to be a homemaker. I am living an extraordinary life being able to stay home. I love my home, family, etc." You can add the rest.

When you take this kind of posture, your conversations will change your posture, making you stand more upright and confident.

It's Your Time Now, Mama!
Copy this truth once a day and scream it out loud!
TRUTH: I deserve to be treated well because God made me to be treasured!

(Deuteronomy 7:6) *"For you are a people holy to the Lord your God. The Lord your God has chosen you to be a people for his treasured possession, out of all the peoples who are on the face of the earth"*

What toxic behavior have you display lately?

List a few boundaries you need to put in place

List some ways you can reposition your thoughts to have a better outlook on being a stay-at-home mom?

It's Your Time Now, Mama!
Unload your mind and then pray about it!

PRINCIPLE SIX

GIVE YOURSELF PERMISSION TO LIVE THE LIFE YOU HAVE BEEN CALLED TO LIVE

Stay-at-home moms, permit yourself to live the life you have been called to live. Too often, we allow society to put us in a box and make us look down at our hard work. We have given in to the world's standard and not the word of God's standard, which far outweighs what others may or may not think of you. The principle of permitting yourself to live the life you have been called to live is critical for fulfilling the mandate of your life.

Giving yourself permission to dream again means allowing yourself to block out the noise or chatter of others. It is essential that you don't waste your time on naysayers because they might not take the leap of faith to go after their dreams.

When you give yourself permission to dream again, you break the limitations you have placed on yourself over the years. You have one life to live, and life is not a dress rehearsal – it is real, and it will go by fast.

Don't go through life with regret because you may think others are thinking of you or even because of what you are presently going through.

Have you ever asked yourself what your life would be like or look like if you decided not to care what others thought of you?

Have you asked yourself what would happen if you went through life without any fear and moved courageously?

Remember how, when you were a child, you used to sit down and think about what you wanted to become or which country you would travel to?

Stop right now, go back to your childhood days, and let those moments sweep over you.

I can imagine the joy that floods your heart and the smile or tears on your face.

God wants you to DREAM again!

I don't know what that dream was, but one thing I DO know is that the same dream is STILL possible. So that dream that is still locked up in your mind is possible.

Sometimes your present situation makes it hard to say that it is possible, but these situations will pass. Though they bring about setbacks and you may feel defeated, they will pass.

God has placed those dreams and ideas in your heart as a part of your journey here on this earth.

We tend to make a permanent decision in a temporary situation. When you are in a season of your life where your children are young, and you have little time or no time to keep up with yourself, it is easy to fall into the trap of continually remaining that way.

Soon, we lose ourselves along the way and stop pursuing our dreams. Several years ago, I got caught up in raising the children, being a wife and a mom.

Along the way, I forgot who I was.

I began to settle and stop pursuing what the Lord placed on my heart.

I was going through the everyday chores and the next item on my to-do list. Apart from praying and reading God's word, there was nothing really to look forward to each morning.

Every turn you take in life, there will be distractions from the moment you open your eyes until the time you rest your head on your pillow. There is always something to pull you away from your heart's desire.

As I talk with stay-at-home moms daily, I hear the deep inner cry of what they wanted to become or the question of, "Why did I stop being myself?"

One Friday night, my daughter had one of her friend's sleepover, and I had a conversation with her friend's mother the next day.

"What was it that you wanted to become before having children?"

She paused for a moment, then she said, "A nurse or Doula, and Childbirth Educator."

"What is stopping you from doing that?"

"Well, I need to order my transcript and send it to the school, but I have not gotten a chance to do so." It had been over a couple of years of not getting the chance to order it. I then looked her in the eyes and said, "No more excuses, get that transcript and get moving because time is not waiting for you".

A few weeks later, I saw her again, and she was registered to be a Certified Doula and Childbirth Educator. Unfortunately, this mom had stopped dreaming and pursuing her passion because of the many distractions she had in her life.

Don't get me wrong-- it's not easy, but it was possible to have her heart's desire and still be an amazing wife, mom, friend, etc.

Ladies, you must be willing to go after your dream and make it happen. It took me almost thirteen years to complete my Bachelor's in Psychology in Life Coaching. Why? I can relocated; during my journey, it was challenging, but I chose not to give up. Over the years of studying and having children, three times out of my seven pregnancies, I had stillbirths. During these challenging times, we were still homeschooling our children.

Even with all of this, I was determined not to quit despite what life threw my way.

Was the journey easy? NO!

Are the excuses valid? Yes, but in this heart of mine, excuses weren't going to be a crutch, neither were they going to stop me.

Giving yourself permission to dream again means forgetting the past failures.

There are some of you who have tried going after your dreams and, because of what was going on in your life at the moment, you made a permanent decision not to pursue your dreams again.

There are some of you who failed several times and decided that's it. The truth is that things will always happen in your life no matter what, but how you react to those events will affect future choices. Beautiful, the past is the past, and reliving the past each day of your life will not allow you to take one step in the future.

If you are reading this book, this means you need to step away and disconnect from your past and permit yourself to LIVE for the present and future.

There are many great adventures that await you. So whether you have made that decision not to move forward one, two, or ten years ago, it's time to let it go and move forward boldly. Following and fulfilling one of your dreams may lead to fulfilling others' dreams you have always had.

I ran from writing this book for many years because I made and found excuses day after day. Finally, one day, I decided enough is enough and said that I am just going to just write.

I know there are mothers who are dying inside because that void inside their hearts needs to be filled; therefore, my dreams are tied to millions of moms who need to be encouraged with a gentle kick in the butt to get moving.

Remember that your children are watching you each day. When you choose not to do anything with your life, you are molding them to follow in your footsteps. Why not follow your dreams?

The Lord has placed a wide door before you to become who He has called you to be. In the book of Revelation 3:8, He said, *"I know your works. Behold, I have set before you an open door, which no one is able to shut. I know that you have but little power, and yet you have kept my word and have not denied my name".*

Giving yourself permission to dream again is allowing yourself to walk through the door which is provided for you. Don't let another day, week, or month pass you by without shaking off the dust of the past and moving forward.

Moms, your life depends on it!

Your life is like a canvas. What will you paint? As you wake each morning, you don't know what the sky will paint for you throughout the day.

The weather forecaster may predict rain and not even one drop of rainfalls.

They may predict a sunny day, and to your surprise, the sun had to fight its way to shine through the clouds, but you can decide what you want your day to be like.

You are the forecaster in your day; decide what your canvas will display each day and paint it.

Now, you were born with those dreams and desires locked up in your heart and, if you don't put them on this canvas, then who will?

Ladies, you are given the opportunity to be the masterpiece you are created to be. What will your house look like if you start to run after your passion, or how different will it be in your home? After coaching one of my stay-at-home moms over two months to do just one thing towards her dream daily, she finally realized that the atmosphere within their home changed dramatically.

"Because I decided to start studying to finish my Master's in Accounting, I became so happy. Of course, it is stressful at times, but

I am happy. My children even asked, 'why are you so happy these days, mom?' I am lost for words".

Moms, even your children can see you are not yourself when you stop dreaming. They can see that you are not as happy although you wear a smile every day.

As homemakers, we set the tone in our homes and, when something is lacking within our hearts, although we try to hide it, it will still be exposed one way or the other.

It's easy to persuade yourself out of your dream without even questioning why you are doing so. However, time will pass by quickly, and things change rapidly. So, homemakers, stop remaining faithful in cheating yourself out of your calling.

You can set aside and watch others progress in their career and often wish that was you, not realizing the choice could be yours.

Not allowing yourself to sit quietly and dream of what you would like to do, apart from loving your husband, children, or family, is cheating yourself and becoming a lesser you. Once, I was talking to one of my friends, who is a stay-at-home mom of four beautiful children, ages 11, 10, 8, and 6. She is busy with her young children, running from one activity to the next.

As I sat down and began to talk about life and how fast our children are growing, I could see and hear some missing pieces from her story.

"If you had to do your life all over again, how would that look for you?"

"You know I would pursue my dream to become an Interior Designer first, then start having children. I love my children, and I would not trade them, but I just love designing spaces. I could see myself designing different homes and some commercial buildings, too". I smiled with great joy.

"Why are you not doing this now alongside your children?" With piercing blue eyes, she gazed at me speechless, as though I was crazy. She didn't realize that I get looks like those all the time. Yes, why not do it alongside your children?

Children will see strength and tenacity when they see or remember their mother. They will not just see the mom who chose to stay home with them, but also the woman who is bold, strong, and refused to give up on her dreams. This, in return, will be a huge encouragement to them along life's journey. Your family will see your struggle and your victory too, and this all comes back to you –

start to dream again and put it into action!

It's Your Time Now, Mama!

Copy this truth once a day and scream it out loud!
TRUTH: I can live an abundant life because God calls me to!

_____

_____

_____

_____

_____

_____

_____

_____

_____

_____

_____

List a few of your childhood dreams

As seasons change in your life, which dreams remain the same over the years?

List your 'Excuses' and replace them with your possibilities!

It's Your Time Now, Mama!

Unload your mind and then pray about it!

Mama! Remember with God All Things are Possible!

PRINCIPLE SEVEN

THINK DIFFERENTLY

Everyone's blueprint isn't yours to follow. I hope that you understand that now. I'm challenging you to apply this principle of thinking differently. Think differently about yourself and your life because I don't want you to fall into the trap of being pacified.

The Bible speaks of us having itching ears because we are always searching for something other than what He has prepared for us in our own life. People will have us believing so many lies that we literally begin to starve!

"You're going to be broke if you stay home…"

"How do you deal with not having time to do anything for yourself…"

"Don't you want a job so you can have everything you want…"

"See, that's why I'm waiting to have kids because I could NOT deal with all that..."

"You're wasting your talents sitting at home..."

"You don't need to go back out there. You have everything you need right here at home..."

LIES! That's all these are – lies that the enemy puts into your head so he can trick you into coming down off the wall where God has placed you to stand guard in your home.

You are not broke, because God isn't broke!

You may not have the material things that you see other individuals have, but you can also rest in the fact that you're not in the debt that some of them are in, either. You're not throwing money at the problems that come into your household. When your children start to act out and start being disrespectful, you can handle it and reset the tone in your home. You're not crying out to God to help you to afford something that you only bought to impress somebody else! You're not trying to figure out which bills to pay first because you got a nose job or a breast augmentation. You're fine with what God gave you, so why do you think you're broke again? Proverbs tell us not to fret because the wicked prosper...remember that! And, that He will supply all our needs!

You have all the time you need to get what you want in life done. The problem is that you are so busy making sure that everyone else has what they need that you are afraid to regulate your household! You are tired and don't want to do anything for yourself because the perfectionist nature that you have won't let you establish a chore chart so that your kids can help you maintain the house.

You sit at their practices, bored out of your mind because you don't see that you could use this moment to read that book you bought three years ago, which is still in the bag with the receipt in it! You don't see the downtime that you have where you can use a few minutes of the day to do something for yourself.

You start to think that a job is an answer to our family's needs, but it's because you've become complacent and lazy, which has caused your house to crumble. So, you figure that the only way to set things right is to get a job. What happens if getting a job makes things worse? Now, you're doing damage control because it became more chaotic to have the job! Will there be times where this will be a legitimate thought? Yes, but there are ways to do it where you don't lose your family! Let me tell you about one of my dearest and craziest friends.

She tells people that she "writes her way through life," ...and she's telling the truth. She has written over one hundred books since September 2015, but that's not what I want to talk about. Her first book came at a time when her family was in dire need. They had gone through a tough transition that left them broke. When the book was published, she begged her husband to give her the money to buy twenty-five copies of the book. She posted the book on social media and quickly filled her pre-order list, with some people buying as many as six copies!

The weekend the books came in was a busy one. There were cars in and out of their driveway and she was in and out of the house delivering books in between. When the dust settled, she had DOUBLED the money that she spent getting the books, and her family was able to make it until the next payday.

Are you paying attention yet? She took a skill she had, marketed it online, got some interest, and made money – all without leaving her home or her family! So, stop thinking that you have to leave your home to make something significant happen for you and your family! Speaking of your family, understand that, because God has a purpose and a plan for your life, having a family will only ENHANCE that!

Having a family, no matter what pre-existing conditions exist, will NOT stop what God has for you. Your family is there to help you, but you must get out of the comfort zone of just making them happy and set the tone for your home! Think about the "Yes, but" and "No, but" concepts. You are letting them know that their needs are important, but yours are too!

"Yes, we can play a game together, but I would like to finish reading this chapter first."

"No, we can't do that today because Mommy has some things she needs to catch up on, but when I am finished, we will see what we can do."

Another thing I want to say about family is this: they are not the distraction you think they are. Have you ever thought that they may be getting under your skin because, as I said earlier, you won't let them help you? Them being in your face and all over you is their way of saying, "Mommy, if you show me what to do, I can help you!" The problem is that you are so wrapped up in being superwoman that you will dismiss that. You will tell people that you never have time, but you don't use those steal away moments we talked about earlier - that time you're under the hairdryer at the salon, that time you're sitting and waiting on them to come out of school or practice, that time you're standing in the checkout line at the store – you have more time than you think!

I can't stand to hear a stay-at-home mom being called a waste of talent, but I love to see the naysayers be proven wrong.

I imagine you decorating your home with one-of-a-kind creations made by your hands.

I imagine you making the clothes that the naysayers wish they could find in a store.

I see you cooking food worthy of being in a restaurant, but it's a meal that you learned to make growing up at home.

I know how they look at you when you are unbothered by what they think because, even with all that they stress themselves out to get done, you're making things work, and they can't understand how because it's not meant for them to understand.

Your home is a well-oiled machine on a good day, and they're coming to YOU for help to maintain THEIR chaos!

One other trap I don't want you to fall into is thinking that being a mom is all that you will ever be! God did not give you talents for you to sit on, and home isn't the only place He wants those talents to shine! They are meant to be shared with the world, and there are myriad of ways to let people know who you are, what you can do, and how you can help them!

Your zone of impact is wherever the soles of your feet rest at any given moment, so what are you doing with that? It's time to think differently.

Lastly, home is your place of peace and serenity, yes, but it is not your be-all and end-all, at all! If you have everything you need, it's time for you to show what you have and be a light and help someone else. It's not a time to get all you can and can all you get.

Even a sponge has to be wrung out every once in a while to remain useful!

Which other stay-at-home mom are you helping to reach her fullest potential in her home?

What are you showing your children – to be a help to those around them, or to be a hoarder and stingy?

If you want people to think differently about you, you must think differently about yourself first, my friend!

It's Your Time Now, Mama!
Copy this truth once a day and scream it out loud!
TRUTH: I am changing my thoughts because God has so much more for me!

(Romans 12:2)
Do not be conformed to this world,[a] but be transformed by the renewal of your mind, that by testing you may discern what is the will of God, what is good and acceptable and perfect.

_____

_____

_____

_____

_____

_____

_____

_____

_____

_____

_____

_____

_____

_____

_____

_____

_____

_____

_____

_____

What pattern of thinking has held you back from not fully embracing your dreams?

_____

_____

_____

_____

_____

_____

List the adjustment you need to make to take the first step towards your dreams.

It's Your Time Now, Mama!
Unload your mind and then pray about it!

_____

_____

_____

_____

_____

_____

_____

_____

_____

_____

_____

_____

_____

_____

_____

_____

_____

PRINCIPLE EIGHT

YOU ARE CHOSEN TO CHANGE THE NEXT GENERATION

The eighth principle is very important for the advancement of the kingdom of God. From Genesis to Revelation, God always saves a remnant so that his words pass from one generation to the next. God has chosen you, stay-at-home moms/dads, to do this fantastic job. However, many stay-at-home moms have that bitter Naomi syndrome. They think that they should give up on being a light and inspiration to anyone else just because they don't have certain things. Yet, Titus tells us that the aged women are to teach the younger women. So, yes, you are indeed chosen to change the next generation. If you're not trying, then you are not fulfilling a major part of your mission from God.

The Bible tells us that we are to live and act in a way that our children and those who come after us will set their hope in God. How can they do that if we are acting like Mara, the name Naomi wanted to be called?

Think about those family traditions that you grew up with as a child. You may not have understood back then, but you do now, and you pass those same traditions on to your children with a little bit of your own spin on it. The memories that come from that will shape generations to come. You have a tremendous responsibility that you shouldn't take lightly!

What you show to your family and to the world everyday matters, so are you living and working in excellence in your home?

What will your children tell your grandchildren about you?

Will they believe what they say?

A son wanted to know his family history, and his mother told him how every man in his family was in the ministry and preached the Word of God, but as the young man looked at these men, that's not what he saw! Instead, he saw them smoking, drinking, womanizing, and more – he knew that this couldn't be what God meant for his service. The women in his family did the same — acted like saints on Sunday, but it was all gone before they left the church parking lot. The Apostle Paul praised Lois and Eunice, the mother and grandmother of Timothy, for being the right type of influence on him.

From the time he was a child, he was taught the ways of God, and they stayed on him about it, too! These women had a standard of God in their lives that passed on to him. Look at what God did with Timothy, the next generation.

Before Lois and Eunice were Hannah, who prayed for a child to raise so that she could train him to serve the Lord. Samuel became a mighty man of God, but it started with Hannah having a prayer life that moved the very heart of God.

Think about Elizabeth, the mother of John the Baptist, who had very strict instructions from God to follow in carrying him and even in naming him! Thus, John became the predecessor of our risen Lord!

All these women had something in common – they understood the children they carried and the responsibility of raising the next world changers! In essence, these women understood the principle of "You are chosen to change the next generation."

Ruth stayed with and listened to everything Naomi told her. From her bloodline came King David, Solomon, and Jesus Christ Himself – all because she took her role as a mother and influencer seriously! They understood what being a light in the world meant long before Jesus said it in Matthew.

The power that you have to impact someone's life is one that many misuses today.

It's not about control, but influence, and there is a difference!

The life that you live today is meant to have a ripple effect, not a domino effect. Yes, you will go through things to get to your mountaintop, Mama, but you shouldn't want that for your children nor theirs. The buck needs to stop with you!

Generational poverty does NOT have to be your legacy!

It's okay for your children to have life skills that don't depend on something electronic. Teach your children how to really survive – plant a garden, teach them to write a letter, how to fill out a paper application. These are lost skills today, and people think that they are outdated, yet if we are honest, we're seeing the need for them more and more as things get worse in our world.

It all starts with you living intentionally before your children. Then, your children will see you model the goodness of God through whatever season in your life.

Teach them early that it is God Who gave you the power and the ability to do all that you do.

Let them know that they came from a mighty and all-powerful God

Who has a purpose for their lives, too.

Express to them the importance of having a real relationship with God and what that means.

Take the Bible and show them how God handles fake and empty relationships with Him.

Help them to see how to reap the blessings of God on their lives once they come to know Him as Lord and Savior!

Changing the next generation means that you take what God has allowed you to do in and with your life and pass it on to them. Those gifts, skills, and talents that you have can be taught to your children and make their lives a little easier in this crazy world we live in.

Think about how many times you have gone back to something that your mother, grandmother, or aunt taught you – the same will go for them one day.

Changing the next generation means that you set boundaries, enforce them, and don't take any mess! Say what you mean and mean what you say. You must Have your game face on at ALL times!

Make them EARN the things that they ask you for.

Teach them the value of hard work and how to spend and save appropriately, even if you have to learn together!

Teach them how to read people and discern who is honest and who is not.

Don't let them grow up green and not knowing anything—the devil will get a hold of them very quickly!

Changing the next generation means that you show tough love when it is necessary. Please stop trying to fix the messes that they make. Teach them that there are consequences to their actions that they will have to deal with. It's not your job to get them out of every little hole they dig for themselves. It would help if you let them learn from their mistakes and develop the integrity and fortitude to do things differently the next time they are faced with that situation.

Changing the next generation means that you express to them the importance of advancing their education, but not at the expense of their relationship with God! Teach them that their service to the Lord through their education does not end once they graduate from high school. That's when the real education begins, and they will need to understand that what God has for them is what will carry them and help them combat what the world is going to try and push down their throats. They need to know how to stand wherever their education may take them. ***Changing the next generation means that you***

protect them, but not overprotect them. There are some things in life that they will need to go through with your guidance.

They are going to mess up.

They are going to get involved with the wrong person.

They are going to get hurt in a relationship.

You can't shelter them from everything and don't fall into the trap of thinking that they won't rebel because they will if you push them too far. You can be strict without damaging their individuality!

Finally, changing the next generation means that you spend time on your knees, laid out before God praying for them. Call them by name. Call their friends by name.... their teachers...anyone around them. PRAY!

The Bible says in James 5:16 "...*The prayer of a righteous person has great power as it is working*" for a reason! You're here because someone was laid out on the floor for you. Somebody prayed in their closet for hours on end for you. Somebody knelt at their bedside and prayed until their body ached for you. It's time to return the favor.

Change the next generation.

Become the Confident Homemaker that God has destined you to

be and let no one but HIM stop you on your journey.

May God bless and keep you as you live the life He has called you to live unapologetically, by His spirit, and with His freedom.

I love you!

It's Your Time Now, Mama!

Copy this affirmation once a day and scream it out loud! Affirmation: I am called to change the next generation because God wants me to have an impact!

_____

_____

_____

_____

_____

_____

_____

_____

_____

_____

_____

_____

_____

List ways you change the trajectory part of the next generation in your household.

_____

_____

_____

_____

_____

_____

_____

_____

_____

_____

_____

_____

_____

_____

_____

Set up small goals to help keep you on the right part to change the next generation.

It's Your Time Now, Mama!
Unload your mind and then pray about it!

Sugie Martin is a dynamic Mindset & Confident Coach. She inspires, uplifts, and encourages busy Kingdom-minded homemakers / Stay-at-home moms/dads to help them create the right mindset to regain their confidence and walk into the calling God has placed upon their lives. Assisting homemakers provide a massive shift in their homes and business and give them the confidence and support needed to pursue their dreams while taking care of your home.

Sugie has been a homemaker and homeschooler for over 17 years. She holds a Bachelor in Life Coaching in Psychology and is the founder of The Confident Homemakers. Sugie has been on several radio interviews internationally, talking about the importance of being a Confident Homemaker and embracing what you have been assigned to accomplish, along with homeschooling strategies. She is married (Dr. Dean Martin), with four exceptional children Tahira, Samuel, Jonathan, and Malachi.

www.ingramcontent.com/pod-product-compliance
Lightning Source LLC
Chambersburg PA
CBHW051945160426
43198CB00013B/2309